D1142602

FOOTBALL SKILLS

TOP THAT! Kids™

Copyright © 2007 Top That! Publishing plc
Tide Mill Way, Woodbridge, Suffolk, IP12 1AP, UK
www.topthatpublishing.com
Top That! is a Registered Trademark of Top That! Publishing plc
All rights reserved

❶ Contents

Nobody knows exactly when football was first played, but some people believe it began in China over 2,000 years ago.

The Early Days
In Britain, children were playing football at least 900 years ago. The game became so popular that, in 1349, King Edward III tried to ban it because he was worried that young men were spending too much time playing football and not enough practising their archery.

Football League
In England, the game as it is played today started in the 1880s, when the Football League was formed.

Popularity
It's now the most popular game in the world and is played in virtually every country. The best players, like David Beckham and Ronaldo, are paid millions of pounds to play each year.

Become a Champion
By mastering the skills described in this book, you'll soon be on your way to being a very good player yourself! Perhaps one day you might even be good enough to play in the World Cup.

One of the great things about football is that you hardly need any kit. All you really need is a ball and somewhere to play, but if you want to look really good, you'll need the following.

shirt

Shirt

Sport shirts are designed so you can run around in them. Why not get one in the same colour as your favourite team?

shorts

Shorts

You will be doing so much exercise, it is sensible to wear shorts, as they will stop you from getting too hot.

Gloves

If you're a budding goalkeeper, you'll need gloves to help you grip the ball and take the sting out of powerful shots.

gloves

MULTI GRIP

DYNAMIC CUT

4

Shin Pads
You wear these inside your socks to protect your shins. Someone might accidentally kick you when they are trying to tackle you.

Football Boots
You will be able to kick the ball further with football boots on and they will help to protect your feet from injury.

Long Socks
You need to wear long socks, because they will help to keep your shin pads up.

shin pads

football boots

long socks

Remember – you may need to mark out a goal, so if you have a couple of cones, you can place them a few feet apart. If not, a couple of jumpers will do just as well.

Before you start playing football – or any sport, for that matter – you need to warm up. If you don't, you run the risk of serious injury as your body won't be ready for sudden bursts of speed, or stretching to reach a ball.

Warming Down

Warming down is just as important as warming up, so make sure you do a few light stretches after you've practised, too.

Under Ten

If you are aged ten or under, you're lucky, because you should be naturally fit. Just a few simple swings of the arms, a twist of the hips and a quick jog should be all you need to loosen up.

Ten to Twelve

If you're aged between ten and twelve, there's a bit more you can do to get ready for a game, but make sure you don't overdo it. Your warm-up should only last about ten minutes.

Pro Tip
Start your warm-up with a gentle jog around the pitch.

The Warm-up

First, do some gentle jogging to get rid of any cobwebs and get the blood pumping. Follow this with some stretches, which you should hold for five seconds. Try these ones for size:

2. Now, sit down, stretch your legs out and try to touch your toes. You should feel the muscles in the backs of your legs – your hamstrings – pulling.

3. Stand up again, bend one leg behind you until it touches your bottom and hold it with your hand so you're standing on one leg. If you lose your balance try holding your ear with your other hand – you'll be amazed, but you'll stop wobbling!

4. You can also loosen your neck and your hips by SLOWLY turning them around in a clockwise and then anticlockwise motion.

I. Touch your toes, keeping your legs straight. Try to get the palms of your hands on the ground.

Shuttles are excellent for increasing your stamina and helping you to make it through a full match. They involve running from one point to another, stretching different muscles as you go.

Crazy Cones

1. Use whatever you can (cones are ideal) to mark out points a few metres from each other in a line. Start from the first and run to the furthest away. Pick up the marker and run back to the first marker, dropping your marker on top. Repeat this for the next furthest marker, then the next and so on. If there are enough of you, why not make it into a race?

2. Now, with the markers in a line again, try skipping sideways, bringing your feet together each time.

When you reach a marker, turn around and do it the other way.

3. This time you need four markers in a line. One circuit means running to every marker once and back, so make sure you pace yourself sensibly!

4. For this exercise you'll need more space and a friend with a whistle. Accelerate to a fast sprint until the whistle is blown, then change direction and sprint off again. Change direction at every blast of the whistle.

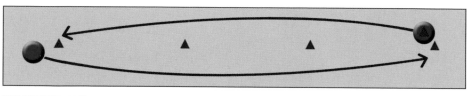

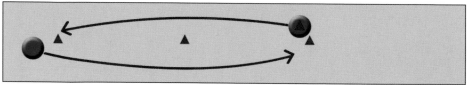

When You Are Running:

Circuit 1
Bring your knees up as high as you can.

Circuit 3
Jump up to head an imaginary ball every time you reach a marker.

Circuit 2
Hold your hands behind your back and bring your heels up to hit them.

Circuit 4
Jog to each marker backwards – but watch where you're going!

Fitness Fun
This last drill is a good one if you're training as a whole team. Remember, someone will have to act as the coach.

1. Find a partner and then get on their back.

2. Now form one big circle, giving each pair a number.

3. The coach shouts out a number and everyone who is on someone's back jumps down and runs around the circle until they get back to their partner.

4. They then crawl through their legs and get into the piggyback position again, but this time it's their partner's turn to be carried.

5. The coach can give a forfeit to the pair who finish last!

On the field, the ball should be your friend, not a hot potato that nobody wants, so it's important to spend some time getting a feel for the ball.

Best Foot Forward

Spend a bit of time tapping the ball up in the air with your best foot, keeping it up for as many reps as possible, then try changing to your weaker foot. Next, use your thigh to juggle with the ball. Then, if you're feeling really confident, you can even use your head!

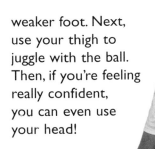

Juggler

Don't worry if you can't keep the ball up for very long — by the end of this book you'll be juggling with the best of them!

Be Accurate!

Choosing the right part of your foot with which to kick the ball is absolutely vital as it will affect the accuracy and the pace of your pass or shot. Being able to kick the ball well, often under pressure, may be a basic skill, but it's one you will use a lot more in a game than any fancy tricks, so it's worth getting it right!

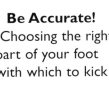

ⓘ Fancy Footwork!

Instep

The most accurate way of kicking a football ball is with your instep, as it allows you to combine power with accuracy and also helps you 'lift' the ball. You'll use your instep when you chip the ball, try a long pass, or take a corner.

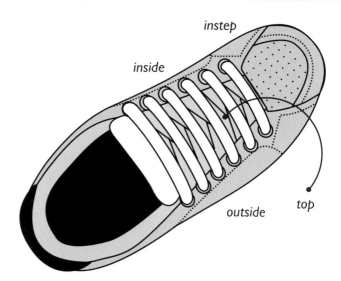

instep

inside

outside   *top*

Inside and Outside

The inside of your foot is good for low passes or for placing the ball. When you use the outside of your foot, the ball will naturally curl. This can be a bonus, but it also makes it harder to send the ball in the direction you want it to go.

For sheer power, use the top of your foot – some coaches refer to this as the 'laces'. Whenever you need maximum power – whether taking a goal kick, clearing the ball, or perhaps having a shot at goal – this is the option to go for. You can also use your heel for passing – but more about that later.

Pro Tips

You will need to master kicking with all the different parts of your foot and here are some general tips worth remembering:

- Keep your eye on the ball.
- Keep your head down and over the ball.
- Don't kick with your toes!
- Know where you are kicking the ball.
- Don't forget to think where your non-kicking foot is – it should be next to the ball when it's struck, as this affects your balance and the power you get.

Key Skills

Part of foot	Benefits	Use
Instep	power & accuracy combined	corners and free kicks
Inside	accuracy	short passes
Outside	swerve	free kicks
Top	maximum power	clearances and shots

Instep

Top

Inside

Outside

Forget shooting, volleying and free kicks – most of the time you kick a ball it will be a pass to a teammate – hopefully! So learning how to do it properly is quite an important skill!

Awareness

To be good at passing the ball requires two things. First, you need to be aware of what is going on around you.

• Where are your teammates?

• Are they running into an open area?

• Is anyone calling for the ball?

• Are you being closed down by a defender?

Technique

Next comes technique. It doesn't matter how good your awareness is if you don't have good technique.

• How hard should you kick the ball?

• Should it be along the ground or lofted in the air?

• What should you do once you've made the pass?

• Should you be looking for a return?

• Make sure you are concentrating all the time, because lazy passes are usually bad passes.

Weighting the Pass

You'll sometimes hear football commentators say "That was a perfectly weighted pass". In other words, the ball should be kicked firmly, but not so hard that it makes it difficult to control. If a player is running, then you should try to pass the ball in front of them, so they can run onto it.

Pro Tip
Don't just stand there admiring your pass. Think about what happens next. Be aware.

● Side Pass

The simplest pass is the sidefoot pass. It's great over short distances, as long as you get the speed right.

1. The non-kicking foot should be next to the ball, with your knees slightly bent and your arms away from the body to give you balance.

2. When you strike the ball, your kicking foot should be just off the ground and at right angles to your other foot. Try not to lean back, as this may send the ball up in the air.

Passing Practice
This exercise is designed to make you use both feet to pass the ball, although in a game always use your stronger foot if you can. Stand about five metres from your partner and practise passing the ball backwards and forwards using your right foot, then your left. Remember to stay up on your toes and be ready for the next pass.

The 1–2 pass will get you past the toughest defender.

The 1–2
You need at least two of you to practise this, although a third person could act as a defender, marking player B.

1. Use two markers as a goal.

2. Start off by standing at least five metres apart, but facing each other. The move is very simple, player A passes to player B...

3. ...who immediately passes it back to player A. The secret is that the pass is weighted correctly and that player A keeps moving in order to receive the ball.

4. Player A can then run on and have a shot.

Try running in different directions and at different angles to confuse the defender even more, or even try a double 1–2!

Lofted Pass
Outwit the opposition by passing the ball over their heads with a lofted pass.

Make sure your non-kicking leg is alongside the ball and slightly bent at the knee. Your body should be leaning backwards slightly and just before you kick the ball, your head should go up.

Kick the lower part of the ball and make sure that your leg follows through.

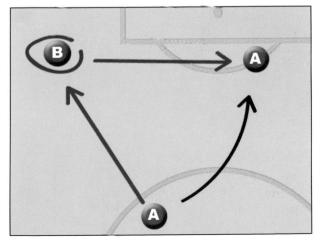

The back heel is a simple, yet effective, way of tricking your opponents – but beware, because you can't actually see where the ball is going, you can easily give away possession.

1. Have a good look around you before receiving the ball. Make sure you control it when it comes.

2. Then, use your heel to send it backwards.

3. You can also use the sole of your foot to roll the ball back – this gives less power, but more accuracy.

Practice

You'll need a partner. Mark out a square. Player A has the ball and starts making a diagonal run across the square. When Player A is halfway, Player B also starts making a diagonal run, but to the opposite corner. Player A must now back heel the ball into the path of player B, but it must be weighted and timed so that player B simply picks the ball up and continues on his run.

The best way to learn the important skill of passing is by practising. Try these drills to make you a pass master!

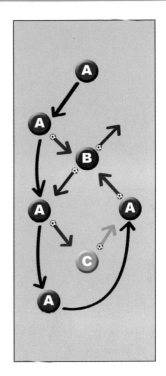

Passing Drill

You need three players for this drill, in a line about ten metres apart.

- Player A runs next to Player B and passes him the ball.

- Player B then passes the ball back to Player A, who then passes it to Player C.

- Player A then runs around the back of Player C, to receive the ball from them on the other side. Player A then passes the ball to Player B and so on.

It sounds more complicated than it is and is great for improving your first-time passing.

Time For Some More Practising!

If there is a big group of you – at least five – then this is a great exercise to improve your passing skills and fitness.

Four of you form a circle, with the fifth player in the middle. The idea is for the player in the middle to intercept the ball as the players in the circle pass it to each other. You can start off with two touches – one to control the ball and one to pass it – but as you get better, try passing the ball first time.

This exercise also gets you into the habit of calling for the ball and letting your teammates know where you are. You might even want to introduce a forfeit for the player in the middle if you complete ten passes – how about some sit-ups? But make sure you take it in turns.

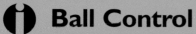 **Ball Control**

Ball control is a great skill to have, as it will give you more options when you have the ball.

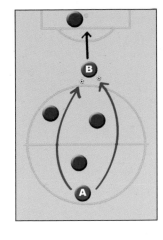

Curving the Ball

This isn't an easy skill to learn, but is a great one to use at free kicks and corners. A curving pass can open up the tightest of defences.

The key thing to remember is that the ball curves in the opposite direction to the side that you kick towards.

Inswing

Kick the outside of the ball with your instep and let your leg follow straight through.

Outswing

Hit the inside of the ball with the outside of your boot and let your leg follow through across your body.

Pro Tip

To get used to this technique, really exaggerate the follow through with your kicking leg.

Crossing

A good cross is a great source of goals, but there is a lot more to it than simply booting the ball in the air in the general direction of the opposing team's goal!

The first choice you need to make is where to aim:

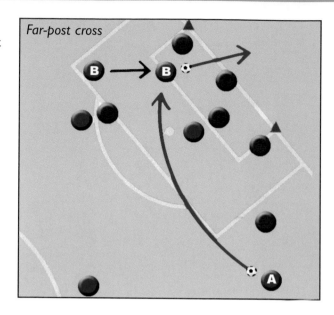

Far-post cross

Near-post Cross

A near-post cross brings with it an element of surprise, as a quick forward can nip in with a header at goal, or even flick the ball on, leaving defenders stranded.

Far-post Cross

A far-post cross puts the goalie under pressure and is great if you've got a tall centre forward charging into the box!

Cutback

Sometimes though, when you get to the goal line, a cross might not be appropriate. Then, you might want to think about passing the ball back to the edge of the area for a teammate to have a shot.

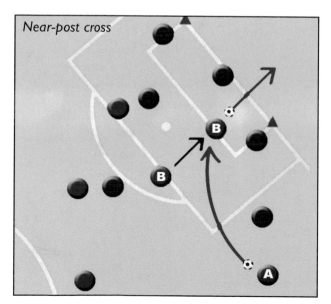

Near-post cross

Technique

1. If you can, when you cross the ball, it's best to try and make sure your body is facing in the same direction as you want the ball to go in.

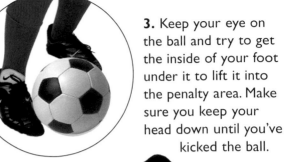

3. Keep your eye on the ball and try to get the inside of your foot under it to lift it into the penalty area. Make sure you keep your head down until you've kicked the ball.

2. Of course, this won't always be possible so your non-kicking foot becomes very important and should be close to the ball to give you more balance.

Practising Crossing

The more players the better for this exercise! You'll need to split up into two teams – one to defend the goal, the other to attack it. Now, take it in turns to cross the ball, varying from near post to far post and try to keep the ball away from the goalie. The attackers should try to lose their defenders, while the defenders must keep an eye on them.

Try the best of ten and then change around.

Goals win games, and every player must dream of scoring the winning goal in a cup final, or finishing up as the league's top scorer. But that's not going to happen without some practice.

Be Selfish

The best strikers are those with an eye for goal who are confident (or greedy!) enough to shoot whenever they get a chance – even if a pass to a teammate may sometimes seem a better option.

Key Skills
- Aim low.
- Always make the keeper work.
- Stay calm.
- You don't always have to blast the ball – think about placing it.

Hit the Target

When taking a shot, make sure you make the goalkeeper work. If you can, take your time and place the ball past the keeper and also, remember that when you shoot, aim low. You might get a lucky deflection whereas whacking the ball too high and over the bar is no use at all.

The bottom line is that goals win games and if you don't shoot, you won't score!

Go For Goal

Pro Tip
The best way to beat the keeper from close range is to kick the ball along the ground, preferably into one of the corners. Keepers are often big guys and getting down quickly is harder than jumping to tip a ball over the bar.

From Close Range

A scramble in the six-yard box, a hopeful prod at the ball – it's a very common way for the ball to find the back of the net. It also means that you always need to be alert and ready for the ball.

Keep Calm

The real secret of making the most of these opportunities is to keep calm. If you've got a chance to score, don't blow it by lashing out at the ball when you can simply side-foot it in. You've got a lot more control over the ball when you take your time.

Practice

1. Ask your partner to pass the ball across the goal to you.

2. Your job is simply to sidefoot the ball between the goalposts.

3. It's better if you've got a keeper, as that gives you something else to think about!

26

From Long Range

The long-range shot is another method of catching your opponents by surprise. A long-range shot must be powerful if it's going to beat the keeper, but as well as power, it requires quick thinking. For long-range efforts, try to aim for one of the top corners.

1. Imagine a player has the ball just inside their half.

2. They look up to see the keeper is off their line, but need to act quickly as a defender is closing in fast.

3. Making sure their non-kicking leg is next to the ball on impact, they strike the ball with the top of their foot.

4. Keeping their eye on the ball they follow through after kicking it and see that the keeper is beaten.

5. Now it's time to celebrate!

Chipping the Ball

Whether you're shooting or passing, being able to chip the ball is a useful skill to have. It can be used to beat a goalkeeper, send the ball over a defensive wall, or set up a teammate in a goal-scoring position.

Although it lacks the power of a long shot, the advantage of the chip is that you can get the ball up in the air very quickly.

Practice

Accuracy is vital with long-range shots. Set two markers up two metres apart, as far away as you can and see how many times you can score.

Go For Goal

Practice

You are in a one-on-one with the keeper. The angle is tight, so your best bet of scoring is by chipping the ball.

1. The idea is to 'stab' at the bottom of the ball with the lower part of your foot, getting your foot under the ball.

2. As always, keep your head over the ball.

3. See how the kicking leg is bent on impact.

4. Try and keep your non-kicking foot just behind the ball.

5. You don't need much back lift or follow through in order to lift the ball over the keeper and into the goal.

Backspin

Stabbing at the ball also creates backspin, which slows the ball down when it hits the ground. This can be useful if you are making a chipped pass into a small space, such as finding a full back as he overlaps down the wing.

Practice

Set some markers out in a circle and then try chipping the ball into the area. As you get better, try using some backspin to get the ball to slow down as it lands.

If there are two of you, why not set up a goal and have one player chip the ball in, while the other practises their heading skills (see page 40). Chipping the ball is often used at free kicks as well – again as a way of catching the keeper out.

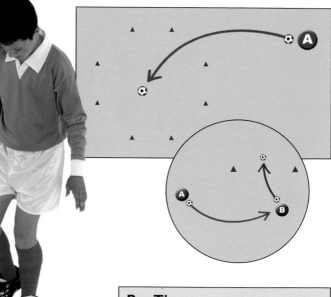

Pro Tip
Once you've decided to shoot, don't change your mind.

Volleying

This is an exciting and often spectacular skill to have up your sleeve, but also a difficult one to master. You can use a volley to shoot, clear the ball or even make a pass.

Power

When you volley the ball you kick it before it hits the ground. If you connect correctly, this is the most powerful way of striking the ball in the game of football.

Balance and Timing

The two vital things to remember are balance and timing. You will need to learn to judge where the ball is going to land and then how to adjust your position. Once again, the non-striking foot will be just as important.

Practice

As with all football skills, practice makes perfect. The volley is great fun to learn, whether on your own or with a willing volunteer to throw the ball into the air for you.

Try throwing the ball against a wall and then volleying it back. With practice, taking up the right position to strike the ball cleanly will become second nature.

Pro Tip

The best volleys are hit smoothly, not snatched at. Make sure you connect with the correct part of the foot to avoid the ball flying off in the wrong direction.

Volleying

Volleying from the Full-on Position

1. The aim is to keep the ball down by getting your head and knee over the ball. This helps the ball go where you want it to.

2. Draw back your kicking foot when the ball is around hip height and keep watching the ball.

3. To get the maximum amount of power into the shot, try to keep your toes pointing downwards, using the upper part of your foot to kick the ball.

Volleying from the Side-on Position

1. Try to get into position as early as possible.

2. You should use your non-striking foot to swivel on.

3. Lean back, using your arms to help you balance.

4. Your kicking foot should come through in an arc – and don't forget that you must follow through!

The Half Volley

This is when you kick the ball as it bounces.

1. It is important that your non-striking foot is close to where the ball bounces to give you extra balance.

2. Keep your eye on the ball.

3. It can be hard to keep down so, once again, you need to keep your knee and head over the ball when you kick it.

4. Of course, follow through when you've kicked it.

Overhead kicks – everyone wants to be able to do them, but practise in private until you're confident enough to show off in front of teammates or spectators!

3. When you hit the ball, aim to make contact with the laces part of your boot.

Take Your Time

Take some time to read about the technique of the overhead kick before you start. This will help you to avoid getting into bad habits which you can't break. It's also very important to study the correct position that your body should be in when you kick the ball, as this will lessen the chances of a bad fall or awkward landing.

Practice

You'll need a friend to throw the ball in.

1. Keep your eye on the ball and try to get your timing right.

2. When you're ready, keep your non-kicking foot on the ground and hook the ball back over your head with your other foot.

4. You will naturally fall backwards, so now think how you are going to land. Try to arch your back and avoid landing flat by spreading your hands to break your fall.

Scissors Kick

A variation on the overhead kick is the bicycle or scissors kick. This is a favourite of the Italian defender Fabio Cannavaro (right). This time, both feet leave the ground, so timing is even more important. When you take off, throw your head back so your body follows – remember, both feet must leave the ground.

Remember!
Overhead kicks can be dangerous for other players as well as you – would you like a kick in the face? So if there is a simpler option, use it.

Okay, so you've learnt one of the more spectacular skills – now back to the basics!

Control

Everyone needs to be able to control the ball and move forward quickly with it at their feet. Done well, a controlled run or dribble can bring the crowd to their feet and create goals that the fans will remember for a lifetime. Some players dribble as if the ball is stuck to their feet with glue!

What You Need

Dribbling the ball needs skill, vision and an awareness of who is around you. At first you'll need to keep both eyes on the ball, but as you get more confident, you'll be able to look up while you're dribbling and decide whether to have a shot or pass to a teammate.

Attack

Being able to dribble well means you can create space and help set up attacks. As you get better, you may wish to add the odd trick to your dribbling to help you throw the defender and get past them more easily. But more about that later.

Don't Overdo It

Dribbling is great, but don't get carried away. Often a pass to a teammate may be a better option than taking on yet another defender!

Dribbling Practice 1

The key to being a good dribbler is to use both feet. At first, it will feel much easier just to use your favoured foot, but try to use both as this is the only way that your weaker foot will get stronger.

This drill is designed to teach you close control, as well as how to run, stop and accelerate with the ball. The idea is that you dribble from one marker to the next with the ball under control – and that means no more than 60 cm from your feet.

Pro Tip

Try crouching slightly while you dribble the ball. This will give you better balance, by lowering your centre of gravity.

1. Set your markers up as shown in the diagram below.

2. Dribble from the first marker to the next one and then stop.

3. Make sure the ball is under control and then accelerate to the next marker and so on.

Dribbling Practice 2

This next drill will help you learn how to turn with the ball. The object now is to dribble in between the markers, like a slalom.

1. Set the markers out so they are roughly the same distance apart.

2. Dribble to the first marker, but this time, instead of stopping, dribble right around the marker, in a circle and then continue to the next one.

3. Start off slowly and gradually try to increase your speed while still keeping the ball under your control.

4. And remember to use both feet.

Dribbling

**Dribbling Practice 3
The Body Swerve**
This is a great way to send a defender stumbling in the wrong direction!

Practice
Set your markers out as shown in the diagram below.

Dribble in between each marker, taking care to keep the ball under control.

Dribbling Practice 4
Now try the swerve on a partner.

1. Approach the defender with the ball on your right foot.

2. Dip your left shoulder and begin to transfer your weight onto your left leg as if going to the left.

3. Then, suddenly shift all your weight to your right and use your left foot to accelerate away.

4. Once you've got your confidence, try changing the side which you fake to.

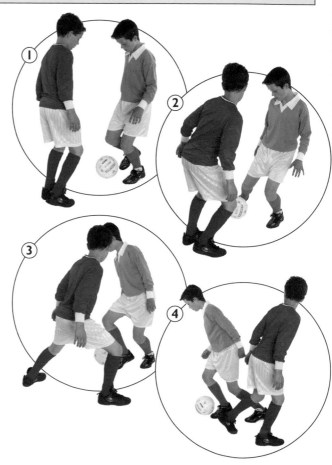

Dribbling

The Step Over

Now it's time to try and use your dribbling skills to beat a defender with a fake. The aim, as ever, is to take your opponent by surprise and send them the wrong way. There are many different types of fakes – but all should be used sparingly or your opponents will get wise to your tricks!

Practice

You'll need a partner for this exercise.

1. Move towards the defender with the ball under control.

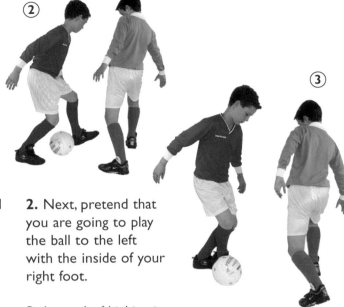

2. Next, pretend that you are going to play the ball to the left with the inside of your right foot.

3. Instead of kicking it, step over the ball.

4. Now pivot on the right foot and, using your left foot, move away to the right.

39

Heading isn't just about making contact with your head – you need to practise jumping high enough to beat an opponent.

Watch the Ball

You will need to keep your balance and watch the ball. If you're a striker, you also need to know where the goal is and make sure that your header is powerful enough to get there.

Technique

First, let's get the movement right: arch your back and thrust your body forwards, moving your head

Size Doesn't Matter

It's worth bearing in mind that you don't have to be tall to be good in the air. Some of the game's best headers of the ball have been well under six feet tall, because heading is about timing and using your whole body, not just your head.

to meet the ball. Use your forehead, not the top of your head, to make contact with the ball and remember – don't shut your eyes!

Pro Tip

When going for a header, shout your name to let your teammates know that you are going for the ball. This should stop them getting in your way. But never shout 'mine', because that's against the rules and it will confuse the other players.

Practice

First, get used to the ball. Try simply bouncing it off your forehead a few times to get a feel for it. Next, throw it up in the air and head it straight in front of you. As you get better, throw it higher and try to head it with more power.

Then, with a friend, practise heading it backwards and forwards between each other. Gradually move further apart so you have to head it harder, but keep your eye on the ball at all times. To get more power into your headers, use your neck muscles. To practise this you'll need a partner.

1. Kneel down and ask them to throw the ball to you.

2. As they do, try to develop a flicking motion with your neck, timing your header for extra power. If you just let the ball hit your head, you won't get any power or distance into

the header.
The next step is to learn how to jump to meet the ball, with both feet off the ground. Although it is better to head the ball when standing, sometimes you will have to beat an opponent to the ball by jumping. Get your partner to throw the ball up and then jump to meet it.

If you are defending, you need to get right under the ball. Push up with your legs just as you head the ball to make it go further and higher. It's a great way of clearing danger.

Scoring

A forward heading at goal needs to head the ball downwards. As you get better, you should think about trying to meet the ball on the move, as this will give your header more power.

Diving Header

If the volley is the most spectacular way to score a goal, the diving header is a close second. It gives the forward an extra edge, an element of surprise and is a great way to get in front of a defender if you are being tightly marked. Timing and courage are the key as you may be at 'foot' level when you've finished, so be careful.

Practice

1. Get your partner to throw the ball in from out wide, as if they are crossing it or taking a corner.

2. You should be almost horizontal when the ball arrives.

3. Try to meet the ball with your forehead – but watch out where you are landing.

Glancing Header

Some players have mastered the art of the glancing header. This is a great way of disguising what you are going to do next. The secret is to use the middle of your forehead – not the sides – and then turn your head just before you head the ball to change its direction.

Practice

If you've got a couple of partners handy then try this exercise.

Three players form a triangle.

1. Player A throws the ball to Player B.

2. Player B then heads the ball sideways to Player C.

3. Player C then throws the ball to Player A, who heads it to Player B and so on. As you get better you can miss out the throw and simply head the ball to each other.

Flick On

You can also use your head to flick the ball on – a ploy often used at near-post corners. Use the speed of the ball to help it on its way. You should be looking straight up at the sky when you've finished.

Although it might all sound complicated, heading does come naturally and you'll find that your body does certain things automatically.

Key Skills

- Use your forehead.
- Keep your eyes open.
- Use your arms to help you balance when you're in the air.
- Don't just let the ball hit you – attack the ball.

The dead ball kick is another part of the game that can bring glory to a player! Free kicks, for example, can be real crowd pleasers, whether a thunderous drive from a long way out or a delicate chip that leaves the keeper flat-footed and looking like a clown!

Other Free Kicks

Of course, not all free kicks result in a shot at goal and some, particularly if taken quickly, are used to catch the opposition unaware and set up attacks.

Shooting Chance

If the free kick is within shooting distance, the opposition will normally form a wall to try to block it. You then have the choice of bending the ball around the wall, shooting over it, or if you feel like being really sly, try a low kick that goes under the wall, as the players' natural instinct will be to jump up to block your shot!

Lay Off

You can also lay the ball off square from a free kick and give a teammate a crack from a different angle away from the wall. Or, you can go for the delicate chip over the wall for one of your teammates to run on to.

To practise this, simply use two markers as a goal and then line the rest up as a wall. Place the ball about five metres away and with practice, you could be a top scorer!

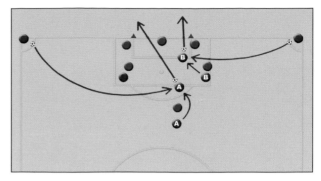

Corners

Corners are great goal-scoring opportunities and can put the defending team under a lot of pressure. They should never be wasted and professional teams will spend many hours practising corners – both offensively and defensively.

Technique

The technique is the same as crossing the ball, but you've got more time to measure where you want the ball to go.

By kicking 'across' the ball slightly, you can generate some spin which makes it harder for the keeper to catch. You can use the outside of the foot to take a corner, but it's easier to use your instep.

You should normally aim a corner for the area just outside the six-yard box. If your team is defending a

corner, it's common to have a player standing on each post.

As with crosses, you can also go for the near or far post. Or, in order to change the angle, you can play it short to a teammate who then whips the cross in. This also gives your forwards more time to lose their defenders.

Penalties

Your team has won a penalty and you've been asked to take it. You have two choices – do you blast it or do you place it?

To place a kick, you use the side of the foot, placing it out of the

reach of the keeper into one of the corners.

Whatever way you choose, the experts believe that the best place to put a penalty is low and just inside the base of the post.

If you're on your own, you can still practise penalties. Just use two markers for goalposts and then put two more markers just inside the posts. The aim is to hit the inside markers.

To blast a kick, you use the top of your foot. You get more power this way, but also run the risk of seeing the ball sail over the bar!

Back heel Using the back of your heel to kick the ball.

By line The line which marks out the end of the field.

Corner An indirect free kick awarded to the attacking team when the ball goes behind the goal and the last player to touch it was a defender. It is taken from the corner of the field nearest to where the ball went off.

Crossing Hitting the ball across the field, usually from the wide areas into the centre.

Dribbling Running with the ball controlled at your feet.

Free kick A set kick, awarded after a foul. Direct free kicks allow shots on goal; indirect free kicks must begin with a pass.

Goal The area of posts, crossbar and netting; also a successful attempt to score.

Half volley Kicking the ball just as it bounces.

Header A pass or attempt on goal using your head.

Instep The part of your foot to use for accurate and powerful kicking.

Inswing Curling the ball inwards.

1–2 A type of pass.

Outswing Curling the ball outwards.

Overhead kick Kicking the ball over your head. One foot remains on the ground.

Passing Giving the ball to a teammate.

Penalty area The goalkeeper's area and the only place he is allowed to handle the ball.

Penalty kick A direct free kick on goal taken from the penalty spot and awarded for a foul in the penalty area.

Reps Repetitions.

Shin pads Protection for your shins.

Shot An attempt to score.

Side pass Sidefoot pass.

Warm up Preparing your body for hard physical exercise.

Tackle An attempt to win the ball from an opposing player using a foot or leg.

Teammate A player on the same side as you.

Scissors kick Like the overhead kick, except both feet leave the ground.

Six-yard box Area inside the penalty box within six yards of the goal.

Step over A trick to use when dribbling in order to send the defender the wrong way.

Volley A shot or pass made before the ball touches the ground.

Wall A line of players standing together. Used to defend free kicks near the goal.

To Find Out More

There are many places to go if you want to get more involved in playing, or if you just want to find out more about the sport.

Clubs

There's bound to be a football club near you that runs junior football teams. Call them up and ask if you can come and have a look, taking your mum or dad with you. If you like the club, you're sure to be welcome and, if you're good enough, you'll soon be in the team!

Websites

If you want to look on the Internet for facts about new skills or even your favourite team, ask an adult to help you. Just type in the information you are looking for into a search engine and you're away. You're sure to hit sites with the latest news and views on the world's most popular team sport.

Two websites you might want to check out are: www.uefa.com, the website for UEFA, the governing body for European football and www.fifa.com, the website for FIFA, the governing body for world football.

Acknowledgements
Key: Top – t; middle – m; bottom – b; left – l; right - r;
Front Cover: www.sporting-heroes.net
1: Allstar. 2: Allstar. 10: Allstar. 13:(m) Allstar. 15: Allstar. 20: Allstar. 25: Allstar. 29: Allstar. 32: Allstar. 34:(r) REUTERS/Dylan Martinez. 37: Allstar. 42:(b) Allstar. 43:(bl) Allstar. 44:(bl) Allstar. 48: Allstar.
All other photos by Top That!